I0532994

Love Made This Happen

A Guide to Harnessing the Power of Love to Transform and Weather the Storms of Relationships

Kemi Emmanuel

Contents

Contents

Acknowledgement

I want to thank my husband, Adewuyi, for allowing me to spend hours into the night writing this rather than talking to him. Thanks for being patient, dear.

I want to thank my daughters, Danielle and Victoria, for their continued support of my book cover and for listening to me read sections of the book to them. They helped make it make sense! Thank you, babies. I also want to thank my son Denzel for encouraging words and gently prodding me along. I appreciate you, son.

I love you all, my beautiful family.

Most of all, I want to thank God for the inspiration, for speaking to me when I just needed to hear this, and for using this book through me to bless the nation. Thank you, Father; I am most grateful.

Introduction

This book was born out of a time in my life and relationship where I found a whole new meaning to the word love. I found I had to keep loving even when I struggled to. I kept wondering why I needed to, and it caused me so much grief. I then had to learn that love was greater than any feeling or emotions I had and as a result I needed to find inner peace, and to do this, love had to be my driving force. I am sure many of you reading this book can relate.

This is about the power of love and how we can harness its power to lead a life of peace and serenity despite all the adversities in relationships.

This book explores love and its meaning. It looks at the different types of love, using ancient Greek philosophers such as Plato and Aristotle's definition, the meaning of which effectively describes what love means. It looks at the different relationships we form and the love that serves as the building block for these relationships.

It explores the difficulties we experience in different relationships and the storms that come with them. When we understand how to weather these storms, we will appreciate our relationships more than ever before.

This book also explores the importance of forgiveness to maintain love in our relationships. It shows how unforgiveness can destroy us and our relationships, leading to anger, bitterness, heartbreak and mental breakdown. But it also shows ways to overcome this and develop a new approach to dealing with hurt and pain.

The book also addresses the fear of the unknown, which is a big part of our relationships and makes us nervous about developing relationships. We explore how this fear can paralyze us and dominate our existence to such an extent that it prevents us from enjoying a peaceful and joyful life. We look at how we can overcome fear and develop the courage to continue a loving relationship and manage our fear to overcome it.

Finally, we define the ultimate love and how this can create a new you that is able to form loving relationships that last despite the difficulties. A new you that is resilient and able to manage emotions using love as a tool. It looks at the ultimate love and how this remains a framework for us to tackle our ever-tumultuous relationships.

I hope you enjoy it and find it thought-provoking and life changing.

Chapter 1

What is Love?

Many have varying ideas of what love means. It is easy to talk about love. It is easy to say, "I met this guy today, and I am in love!" It's easy to say, "It was love at first sight." It's easy to say, "To love and to cherish," before we say I do.

What's challenging to say about love is, "How do I love effectively? How do I maintain these feelings of love? How do I love when all I feel like doing is hate? How do I love the unlovable? If there is someone who can be described as such, in essence, the doing of love is the hardest bit!

The storms we weather in life teach us what love means. We can choose to remain in the storm with love in the boat to help us stay on course or jump out of the ship to start a new journey to find love. Many speak about falling out of love again, but this is a choice. When we understand the true meaning of love, we talk about falling in love, but can we fall out of love?

Learning to love is a journey that starts from birth. The nurturing and love of our parents help us understand the importance of love and relationships. This is described in the "attachment theory" theory if you were trying to put a name to this initial learning about love. The attachment theory describes our innate need to forge bonds with parents or caregivers at birth. John Bowlby (1958), a psychiatrist, was the first to introduce the "attachment theory." He described attachment as a "lasting psychological connectedness between human beings, and early separation in childhood tended to lead to maladjustment in behavior.

Sigmund Freud, a psychologist, on the other hand, suggested infants in the oral stage of their development become attached to the source of pleasure, who at this point is their mother, who fulfills their oral needs. This describes love as pleasurable, and we tend to be drawn to what gives us pleasure from childhood. This type of attachment is created and provides the sense of safety and security that children enjoy, leading us to a more stable adult life.

However, it is sad to say that this loving function is not always achieved at birth, and it often leads us to a quest for love throughout our lives. The truth is love is a choice. You can choose to love or hate, i.e., the opposite of love. This determines your outcomes in life and relationships. Love takes many forms, and to understand love, it is imperative to define the various forms of love. Love is an emotion, a feeling, or an act. You can feel or demonstrate love. Feeling love is what we enjoy the most, as it feels good to be "in love."

Demonstrating love, on the other hand, takes much more than feelings. It takes choice, effort, and understanding of the origin of love.

In many faiths, the origin of love stems from a higher being who, in many ways, demonstrated love for humans by creating them. Maintaining this love is how humans can learn to truly love. The Christian faith and the Bible describe God as "Love" 1 John 4:16. Love is an act of giving but can also be an act of receiving. It is crucial to understand how to give and receive love. It requires understanding how the individual in the relationship provides their love. This helps us accept that love, i.e., the love language, without a different expectation, which, if not fulfilled, can lead to conflict.

Types of Love

The type of love we feel for our various relationships differs and could be the love we feel for family members, which differs from the love we feel for our friends or colleagues. It could be love for our partners, which is romantic and expressed differently. Greek words describe different types of love and has named them as follows:

Storge

Storge ["store-jay"] This is the love we feel towards members of our families. It is the love we feel towards our parents, children, siblings, and extended family members. This love is instinctive and reciprocal and comes from birth. *Storge* love is the fondness born out of familiarity or dependency. We tend to love our families and form bonds that can last a lifetime. However, we can experience difficulties such as sibling rivalries, abuse, or separation in families, and this can lead to severe familial dislike and cause families to produce hateful relationships. The love of our families can sometimes be the most trying of love as we don't have a choice in whom we choose as our family as we are born into this love. This hatred can be transferred through generations; we must be mindful of what kind of love is transported through the family. Our love of our families requires us to be long-suffering because even when you stay away from your family, it does not stop the blood from flowing through your veins. I used to watch a program called Heir Hunters, where probate solicitors find ways to hand over outstanding wealth from one family member to other family members. It amazed me that most of the time, the individual inheriting the wealth of this family member never even knew them as they had been estranged from the family but were receiving their love. It makes me wonder why we stay away from our families in life only to have to demonstrate our love in death. What loving moments have been missed due to bitterness towards our family members?

Ludus

Ludus is the love we demonstrate through flirting and seduction, emphasizing having fun and does not need commitment. This kind of love is currently very rife today, as individuals can no longer see the need to commit to marital relations as necessary. It is casual with no strings attached and can involve sexual relations. This type of love can be temporal and only lasts a flitting moment, such as a one-night stand! This kind of love is usually short-lived and very circumstantial. Many even use flirting techniques to acquire favor in certain circumstances. This flirting technique can also charm us into what we think is a long-term loving relationship. The difficulty arises when a party in the relationship crosses into eros love territory and falls in love, but this is not reciprocated. This leads to heartache and can lead to hatred, abuse, and even mania-style love, where one party can start to stalk the other. While Ludus's love can make us feel good temporarily, it is unsustainable. Many remain on this journey in a quest to find permanent love, which they never do.

Eros

This is sexual or passionate love, which involves romance, sexual desires, attractions, and encounters. We tend to experience eros love and describe this as "falling in love." We demonstrate this love towards our partners, and we express this in both our emotions and the things we do. It often involves physical pleasure, particularly in the early stages of our relationships with our partners and can be very consuming. I watched a documentary once which described being in love as a form of addiction, and one can have withdrawal symptoms when this love is taken away from us. This love can be demonstrated within and outside of marriage. We derive so much pleasure from eros love, both emotional and physical, mainly when it is reciprocal. It can even be so pleasurable for us to watch when we see this demonstrated at weddings or watch romantic comedies. Outside of marriage, this love can be challenging to sustain. The difficulty we can experience in this type of love is when that pleasure no longer exists, and then maintaining and remaining in love becomes a challenge in the relationship. The question then becomes, What next? It can lead to couples describing themselves as falling out of love. I am often baffled as to how couples who appeared to be so into each other suddenly find it hard to stay in the same room, leading to divorce. This can cause mental health difficulties in families. It can be devastating when I come across in my line of work the pain and suffering caused to many due to divorce and the breaking of eros love.

Philia

Philia love is the love felt towards our friends based on shared goodwill. This is your love for your friends, which comes in different forms. This is usually a long-lasting friendship where individuals can share the good, the bad, and the ugly. Some of our friendships are for a season and a reason, while some are based on similar interests and mutual benefits. Sometimes, we have party friends, friends we go shopping with, or friends who are gym buddies. There is a need for companionship between friends and a level of dependency. As friends, we depend on each other, and trust is required to a large degree. If this trust is broken, it can sometimes cause as much heartache as a break-up between romantic relationships. Love in friendships can be short-lived or long-lasting. The difficulties in philia love are that people grow, change, and want different things. I have experienced childhood friendships where individuals describe themselves as best friends but end up hating each other as grown-ups because they want different things, and the shared childhood interests no longer exist.

Agape

Agape ["aga-pay"] is the universal love of God. It manifests itself in our love for strangers, nature, or God. Agape love stands the test of time and does not expect a reward. Demonstrating agape love gives us a feel-good feeling as it is unconditional. To understand Agape love, we can look at the Christian description of love in the Bible.

1 Corinthians 13:4-7 (NLT): *"Love is patient and kind. Love is not jealous or boastful or proud 5 or rude. It does not demand its own way. It is not irritable, and it keeps no record of being wronged. 6 It does not rejoice about injustice but rejoices whenever the truth wins out. 7 Love never gives up, never loses faith, is always hopeful, and endures through every circumstance."*

This kind of love lasts long and is sustainable even when we don't feel like loving in our relationships. The ultimate aim for love is to attain the point of Agape love in our relationships, where we remain in the boat regardless of the storm.

Pragma

Pragma is practical love based on reason or duty. This is the love we feel after we have been married for a long time. It is also found in arranged marriages and develops in many marriages over time. It's no longer about sexual desires but a sense of commitment and a conscious choice to love and remain in a relationship over time. Pragma love promotes a sense of contentment and care for one another. Pragma love allows couples in marriage to sustain their love after eros love appears to have dissipated. This sense of duty keeps marriages going; the concern is more about family responsibilities. There seems to be a sudden rise in the failure of pragma love in many marriages which have lasted a long time. Many couples now prefer to remain single even after 20/30 years of marriage. Some pan after eros love, which no longer appears to exist in their marriages, and sometimes start to have affairs in a bid to rekindle that feeling of falling in love. How long this would last is often questionable, and we see many individuals craving the original pragma love they had done away with and wanting to return to their previous spouses. Some could say it's about the "devil you know." I somewhat prefer the term "the angel you loved." Many, disappointed by their partners, give up on life due to the heartbreak involved.

Philautia

Philautia is the love we feel towards ourselves. This is the most important love because if we cannot love ourselves, we cannot give love to others. The love we have for ourselves can be healthy or unhealthy. Healthy self-love translates into the amount of self-esteem we have and prevents us from self-harming. Unhealthy self-love leads to a lack of self-confidence and self-hatred, making life unbearable. We need to demonstrate Love as God does; the Bible describes us as being made in the image of God, and God is Love, so we must have love for ourselves as we, in essence, are love.

We have much to learn from our Christian faith, which also states that we must love our neighbors as we love ourselves. How can you love your neighbor if you don't love yourself? We need to nurture our relationship with ourselves and ensure it's healthy for our mental health to manage our relationships overall. Self-love requires resilience and stamina to withstand the various storms encountered in everyday life. Most fall due to a lack of understanding of the need to surround themselves with activities that enhance their self-love.

Mania (Obsessive Love)

This love, which I just discovered, has its terminology, but it is very much a part of our communities. This love is toxic and can be referred to in stalking relationships. There is usually an imbalance of power, and one party can become too attached, believing they are entitled to the other party's love even if it is unrequited. When we find ourselves on the receiving end of this love, we become deflated and scared of the outcome. When on the giving end of this love, we can become frustrated and desperate if this love is not reciprocated. This reminds me of the saying, "Love hurts" You are damned if you do or damned if you don't. No one wins in this kind of love. This love can be dangerous and fatal for the giver or the recipient. This kind of love can also be referred to as fanatical. It can be love for a person or cause which can lead individuals to commit atrocious acts. When people feel this love, they are no longer in control of their emotions or actions; no wonder it is referred to as mania!

The various descriptions of love do not stand alone in our quest to define love. It is a combination of all the different aspects of love in relationships that truly defines us. Understanding these definitions helps us navigate the mirage of challenges with which relationships are fraught.

Chapter 2

Difficulties and Storms Encountered in Relationships

Types of Relationships You Create

Parental Relationships

Parental rrelationships are created when we are born. We create a relationship with our parents, who become our first understanding of a loving relationship. We rely on our parents for protection and guidance and the wider family for continuity and learned behavior. We are a product of nature and nurture, as has always been said. We create these family relationships that make or break us. Many who have come from failed family relationships end up struggling with personality issues and issues with regulating their emotions. This highlights the importance of this relationship for society as it helps us develop the resilience to deal with life's challenges. It is also comforting to know that we have families to run back to as support when we struggle with life. This familial love helps us manage the difficulties in the other relationships we experience at work, in friendships, or in society. When we do not experience this love as children, as described in the attachment theory, we create a litany of failed societal relationships. We develop relationships with uncles, aunts, cousins, etc., which happens automatically most of the time because of the inherent familial love we feel for each other.

Relationship with Friends

In childhood, we develop friendships with neighbors and schoolmates. Some of these friendships last long-term, but most fizzle out when there is a house move or when we leave school. These relationships help us deal with our understanding of human exchanges. We argue, fight, quarrel, and learn from each other to develop skills we can use in our work and business. The relationship with our friends can be fun and engaging as we share childhood moments that adults do not understand.

Spousal Relationships

As we grow into adulthood, we start to develop a need for intimacy and companionship with someone with whom we want to share eros-style love, i.e., romantic love. We sometimes fall for someone we feel is our ultimate friend because they fulfill our need for romance and intimacy. This type of relationship often starts by meeting someone either by chance or deliberately through online dating sites or matchmaking friends when we have come of age. Initially, we begin by flirting with one another and having no commitments while we get to know each other. We spend time sizing each other up when we first meet before deciding how far we wish to take the relationship. This relationship doesn't always lead to eros love and can stop at the point of Ludus. The saying "You kiss many frogs before you find Prince Charming" refers to exploring different relationships to find the most compatible partner, eventually leading to commitments like marriage.

Working Relationships

It's incredible to think that, on reflection, this is the relationship we spend the most time in. This is the relationship we cultivate because we work together. This relationship has to be based on mutual respect, whether individuals are in superior positions or otherwise. Most of us work between 8/12 hours a day in our workplaces, which is time spent with colleagues of varying professions. This relationship with our work colleagues is interdependent and reliant on working together on a shared vision of an organization.

As we grow in our working lives, we create many different working relationships. Some last a lifetime and follow us wherever we might go, and some only last for the period you are working together. We never really anticipate what to expect from our working relationships. Most of the time, it's a marriage of convenience. We work together because it is convenient to achieve a common purpose.

Faith-Based Relationships

Our faith-based relationships are relationships formed spiritually by our faith. It is born from a shared spiritual belief in a being or a deity. These relationships often develop in places of worship and are based on trust, believing the person sharing the same faith would follow our principles. In some instances, faith-based relationships can be helpful to us when we need someone to share our emotional trauma with or guide us in understanding the faith. I remember the first time I read and understood the Bible; I had a friend and mentor already established in the faith providing a lot of guidance, and she was the first person I shared my understanding of the scripture with. In faith-based communities, we create new families, referring to each other as brothers and sisters, praying, eating, and celebrating together.

Relationship with a Deity

We develop a spiritual relationship with a deity. The relationship we develop sometimes means we worship a deity we do not see or hear. The Christian faith believes this being is a supreme being who demands our worship. To understand him, we must communicate through prayer and studying his words. He then makes several promises, including the promise of eternal life, i.e., we would live forever, not in our physical bodies but in our spiritual form. We must understand that, as humans, we are made up of body, soul, and spirit, and our spirit lives forever. The body is clay, and we can clearly see this when a body is buried and decomposes. The spirit being behind the body makes us alive and able to operate. This relationship is born out of agape love for the deity we cannot see but who endlessly demonstrates his love for us. We know we are at peace and can weather any storm if we develop this beautiful relationship.

When Love Hurts

Parental Love

This love also challenges our relationships, where we expect so much from family and feel disappointed when this is not actualized. Parents may feel disappointed if their children do not achieve academically or get involved in poor relationships or drugs, leading to grief and shame. Sometimes, familial love can become overbearing and overpowering when parents live vicariously through their children, pushing them to achieve goals the parents could not. This relationship becomes selfish and self-centered around protecting the family business or continuing the family name or legacy. When this does not happen, the relationship breaks down, and I hear people disowning their children. I don't know how you can disown your children if your blood still runs in their veins.

We often hear the saying, "Blood is thicker than water," yet I see children changing their family names because of this relationship breakdown. Individuals may avoid their families and live as though they have no family because of this relationship breakdown. Some children must live with parents who are experiencing mental illnesses and difficulties or living with drug and alcohol addiction. How can you love your parents when this is all you see daily?

I recently witnessed an interview with a young person whose overbearing parents felt they knew what their 20-year-old needed and wanted. While this comes from a place of love, it can negatively impact their relationship, preventing parents from truly knowing their children. Parents are often shocked to learn about their children's actions, and many can swear their children will never do such! As parents, do we really know our children? The child we know at home usually differs from the child the school or friends know.

It is vital to foster an open relationship with our children, so they do not feel comfortable discussing their struggles with us.

We must cultivate friendships and philia love with our children in addition to our parental love. Some children are experiencing bullying at school or going through depression but do not feel they can talk to their parents about this, so they feel at a loss, and they think taking their lives is the only option they have. I hear of many situations where young people commit suicide while their parents are at home because they either feel they have failed them or do not feel confident enough to talk to them about what they have been going through. I recently watched a program where a child killed someone he regarded as his parent because she confronted him about his failures. How many lives are destroyed when this happens? Food for thought, I think.

When a child fails, it's not for us to beat them with a stick and make them feel inadequate. Instead, we should talk to our children, understand, and work together to support the child to improve or do what they like and will excel in. Please remember, not all of us can be doctors or lawyers or engineers like some of our African parents seem to expect. I should not stereotype as I am sure it happens in other cultures too, e.g., Asian culture, maybe. It's incredible how these expectations affect our familial relationships and can create toxic relationships. We need to learn to accept our children for who they are. Not all fingers are equal. This I say, staring at my fingers for confirmation. I am unsure which finger is my favorite or which does the most. Hmm, just some humor in what appears to be a grave matter. I did not think writing this would take me to the depths I have gone, but it is a lot of reflection for me as a child and a parent.

As parents, we need to come to a moment where we allow our children a level of independence and risk and give them the right to choose how they want to live their lives. As parents, we are responsible for loving our children, which is demonstrated in nurture and advice. Still, we are not responsible for living our children's lives for them. I am sure many parents can recognize the difficulties they experience in accepting that children need to make their own decisions. We tend to have countless arguments with our children when we feel disrespected. We wonder why they would not accept our wise decision-making based on our own experience of life. As parents, we sometimes find love in this relationship hard.

On the other hand, children can feel unloved by their parents, especially when overbearing love stems from the stress of conception or being an only child and meaning everything to the parent. If this only child does not live up to expectations, it causes the parent to feel a failure and breaks the relationship. We can also learn our roles and develop our relationships using biblical principles.

Ephesians 6: 2-4 tells us the ideal way for parents to relate with their children. The Bible requests that, as children, we honor our parents so we can have long lives. Still, it also instructs parents not to provoke children to anger or exasperate them by how they treat them.

Unfortunately, many fathers who never understood love (particularly in the African community in which I am from) see the love of their children as purely a disciplinary role. Yes, discipline is necessary, but it does not equate to love and affection, which our children need as they grow under our care. This then affects our relationships, and the long-term effects of this have a detrimental impact on other societal relationships or translate into our relationship with our children.

I once had a friend who refused to have a relationship with his father because he felt all his father did when he was growing up was discipline him. I remember speaking to him once when his father called, and he refused to pick up his call. I remember quoting the scripture on honoring your father and your mother so our days can be extended on the earth. Little did I know that this friend of mine was going to pass away within a few months of this conversation. Now, we might say it's coincidental, or it was his time, but I reflect on how he died. I realized the element of disobedience was a significant factor. Yes, our parents can cause us to get angry and frustrated, but we are still required to honor them, so our relationship with them must still be born of respect.

I also like another verse in the Bible, Prov 6: 20-23, which advises us to obey our father's commands and not neglect our mother's instructions.

I must say the Bible offers numerous verses that help our relationships with our families and members of society. This allows us to remain in love with our family members and create bearable and peaceful relationships between children and parents. We know this love extends to our siblings and our extended families. If we can develop resilience and overlook each other's faults, we can retain our family unit and produce individuals who can manage what society brings our way.

Friendship Love

Friendships play a pivotal role in our upbringing. They help us to navigate society and enable us to socialize effectively. However, some children who are either neurodivergent or come from dysfunctional families can struggle with developing childhood relationships. This occurs when the relationship with the family has not prepared them to understand relationships with others in society. As a result, the individual can become isolated and struggle to make friends as an adult or demonstrate longer-lasting love in friendships. Some become self-centered and selfish in their understanding of life, and even children do not feel the need to consider others' feelings, making it challenging to develop friendships. This can lead to individuals relying on social media for companionship, which can create opportunities for establishing cyber friendships that might lead to fanaticism and radicalization.

Friendships can take on many different dimensions. Some friends are close enough for us to share our deepest, darkest secrets because we trust them. Others we might only share specific moments with, and the friendship doesn't extend beyond those moments. The relationship with our friends can be topsy turvy (an old word). Sometimes, friends can be baffling, and one can struggle to understand them, especially in adult friendships. I know we might sometimes wish we could go back to childhood friendships with no strings attached and no expectations.

Friends go through their own experiences, sometimes translating into how they relate with us. In a recent conversation, I explained some of the difficulties we might have with our relationship with friends. Some friends can be "kind but not nice." It's a strange concept, but on exploration, I found it was characteristic of many friendships I and others I know have had. Kindness is the act of being generous and helpful, and many of our friends tend to be like this. They can come through for us, for example, during major events, but sometimes they are not nice to us, meaning they are not polite or pleasant. They can be self-centered in the way they come across, not considering our feelings. This has broken many friendships where one party feels the other is inconsiderate despite previous acts of kindness that were demonstrated in the past. When this occurs, we tend to have fractured relationships and get hurt by our friends' behavior.

In writing this book, I learned a lot about what this meant for my friendships and how important it was to understand and accept that we are all different, and I needed to love my friends regardless. I learned to walk with them according to understanding, knowing that life might not always be kind to them, and they might struggle to remain nice to you.

It's also imperative to remember that we develop character as we grow, and what you saw as a child is different from what you see now. This helps us manage our expectations. We see friends taking each other's spouses or stabbing themselves in the back for selfish aims. When this occurs, it creates a root of bitterness and anger, which can continue over generations, leaving a wake of hurt and malice. These relationships affect our outlook on life and make trust difficult for humans. We become suspicious of everyone we meet and find it hard to confide in new friends. We must recognize a biblical saying about the heart of man being desperately wicked (Jeremiah 17.9) and consciously try to be nice to our friends or be willing to forgive and love regardless. This, in turn, gives us the peace we need to navigate this world and replaces the bitterness that tends to consume us because of the hurt from friends.

Spousal Love

Spousal relationships are great and can be incredibly rewarding when they work well. They are lifelong and require a lot of strength and resilience from us as individuals. These relationships can be short or long-term, and many find themselves in such courtship for years, believing the result will be marriage. However, this does not always materialize, as some will face heartache when one spouse finds someone else with whom they feel more compatible. It could then seem like wasted years spent with this person amounting to nothing in the end. In some cases, people just find that after courting for a long time, the flirting fizzles away, and the romance and feelings of being in love no longer exist.

The relationship we create with potential spouses must be able to stand the test of time. You must be willing to spend your life with someone whose most uncivilized behaviors you can tolerate. For example, if you cannot stand a man who leaves the toilet seat up or leaves the lid off the toothpaste, please think long and hard before committing to this relationship. It might seem trivial when you are "in love," but over time, it might become very relevant, and you might start to regret why you put up with it.

Similarly, if you feel you cannot stand a woman who spends a long time chatting with friends on the phone and you feel left out because of this, think long and hard before committing to this kind of person. Why are we seeing so many divorces and multiple marriages? It is because over time, in a marital relationship, when the stresses of life, such as work stress, bringing up children, or financial stress, intervene, our patience for each other's flaws starts to wane, and we wonder why we must cope with it. We forget to nurture the most important part of the union, which is "our relationship." We forget that what made us fall in love were the moments we spent alone with each other, the times we spent going out on dates, or the times we spent sharing gifts and playing romantically with each other. How can you maintain a marriage when you only concentrate on the bills or the children? Of course, these are important but when they take the place of your relationship, then you are headed for destruction.

The relationship pitfalls in marriage come in so many guises. A marriage without a solid rock or foundation is likely to crumble. A marriage where couples expect each other to remain the way they were when they met is likely to fail. For example, expecting a woman to remain the same size after having four children is unrealistic, although it is possible for some. It also goes for women expecting their men to maintain six-pack abs after years of hard work and fine dining. In our spousal relationships, we must remember that this is a relationship where two people who have very different upbringings and understandings get together to agree to be relatives for life. This is not like a family relationship where you have no choice; this is a relationship of choice or sometimes not. If choice is not an option in the relationship, then the balance of power is tilted, and what you have is abuse. There is a saying that "if the purpose of a thing is not known, then abuse is inevitable." If we do not know the purpose of our union, then we will start to abuse it. I have seen marriages where couples agree not to have children, or one person agrees to stay at home when they start having children but changes their mind after entering the relationship. It is important to agree mentally and spiritually when entering a union with someone we intend to spend our lives with. If we don't, then the commitment is not total, and we tend to feel we have to leave the union at every hurdle.

These days, we often don't see marriage as a lifetime commitment, and the resilience to stay in the union is often absent. When things don't work out, we feel we can just replace our partner. I am not asking anyone to stay with an individual who uses you as "target practice," beating you to a pulp, and could cause fatal injury; rather, I am saying be alert before entering that relationship. We always need to identify what is holding our union together. Is it the children? The money? Fame? Or the power of love in its various forms. Pragma love is where most relationships end, with a sense of duty and commitment to remain in the relationship because this is what we have always known. It's important to state that the grass is not always greener on the other side. As the biblical principle in Amos 3:3 states, "How can two walk together unless they agree?"

A marriage union is a contract and an agreement with terms and conditions like every contract, and breaching these terms could lead to a variation of the contract terms or termination of the contract, i.e., divorce or separation. This means that people start to act contrary to what the relationship should be about if the agreed-upon terms are not maintained, e.g., to love and to cherish, in sickness and in health, etc. These vows are said, but when it comes to it, I think most struggle to keep to these terms. To be fair, we are human, and human nature wants variety; hence, the temptation to breach the terms of fidelity and faithfulness can sometimes be overwhelming and lead to a breach of trust in the union.

We, therefore, need to create a union based on love. The Bible says that love covers a multitude of sins, and God is love, and his love for us covers our sins. If only we could emulate Jesus, we would find it easier to manage our partner's faults and find common ground where there are none.

It is important to remember that these relationships produce children, and children from broken relationships often face adverse childhood experiences, such as drug and alcohol abuse, mental illness, and domestic violence. These children can grow up as broken adults, contributing to societal issues like crime, mental illness, and homelessness. Food for thought: I encourage you not to be carried away by the eros side of this relationship but to think about ensuring the right foundation before entering this union. Communicate and ask questions, find out each other's plans for the future and agree on them, be ready to accept faults, look out for any red flags, and don't let the infatuation blind you. I believe love can be blind, but only after you have made a conscious effort to make it so. The love that lasts is deliberate. If you are already in a relationship and you think there is no hope, let agape love be your guiding force so you can find inner peace.

Love in Work Relationships

In the context of work relationships, we often feel anxious because we don't know what to expect from our colleagues. Sometimes, it is a choice, and sometimes not. It's even more challenging for those fresh out of college or university and are entering a working relationship with a company based on financial reward. Some remain in their jobs and maintain their relationship for financial reasons, while others see their work as a career opportunity.

Working relationships means spending a lot of time with work colleagues over the week in close proximity, either working in an office or on-site. These relationships can be vertical and hierarchical, with individuals creating relationships with people up the managerial chain. These relationships vary according to your role in the chain and what is expected of you.

Unfortunately, there is often little love lost between colleagues, as many compete for choice positions. For a relationship we spend so much of our time in, you wonder how we manage to remain in such a relationship without tearing each other's hair out. Our work relationship must be civil and formal. We sit in meetings together and share ideas. Many organizations now recognize the importance of team building to ensure colleagues can work together. I have heard many stories of managers being unpleasant to their staff and not considering their feelings. A transformational manager creates a relationship where staff are free to be themselves and can come and speak to them whenever they feel bothered about issues.

Unfortunately, I have seen toxic working environments, and you just wonder how people can work together, spending so much time together, yet hatred is all that is being spewed. Some might find themselves in this relationship at work, and this can sometimes have a long-lasting and detrimental effect on the individual. It can lead to stress and, in turn, anxiety, and depression, with many having to take medication for the rest of their lives or go off sick, which in turn can be costly to both the individual and the organization. There can be incidences of bullying at work, which can affect the love we feel for our work colleagues. There could be feelings of resentment which some colleagues can take out on other colleagues, making the job unbearable.

When you find yourself in a working relationship that is proving unprofessional, or you are under leadership that is unsupportive and critical of your work, it is important to think of yourself. Self-love plays an important role in this relationship. You need to develop resilience, patience, and professionalism. You can love your colleagues without liking them, I suppose—this is where agape comes in. For your own peace of mind, consider whether you want to constantly worry about work or if you are willing to show love and turn the other cheek. This, I believe, is the best approach. Love can help you focus on the positive aspects of your colleagues rather than their negatives.

I am not saying it's ok to accept bullying and harassment in your work relationship. However, the approach we take makes a difference to our own mindset. We sometimes need to love ourselves even if we don't feel loved at work. We must be in a position to have open communication with colleagues with whom we disagree and probably agree to disagree. Making a conscious effort to love work colleagues regardless of differences can contribute to a smoother relationship at work.

Faith/Spiritual love

Relationships, even those based on faith, are not always as ideal as we hope. We forget that these individuals are still human and, like our biological siblings, can disappoint and hurt us. This hurt can be devastating, especially for those not grounded in their faith, leading to some leaving their faith completely. I have seen so many in the Christian faith behave worse than those outside of the faith. I have heard so many say they would never go to church again because of the victimization and abuse they faced in some churches for being different. Instead of embracing people in love and helping them to understand the principles of the faith, they are ostracized and treated badly. How, then, can we fulfill our ultimate commandment, which is to win souls for the kingdom of God? We seem to be losing them instead.

Some people become brainwashed or obsessed with their faith or its leader, leading to mania and radicalization, regardless of the faith. This can have fatal consequences. We must be mindful of the relationships we create in faith communities because people are vulnerable and seeking help.

We do not want them to turn their back on "the faith" completely.

Love for a Deity

While a relationship with a deity can be soul-satisfying and gratifying, I have seen many lose this relationship because of a superficial relationship with the deity or a lack of understanding of how the deity works or expresses himself. For example, in the Christian faith, I have seen many say they are angry with God for letting their parent or child die, and they never want to have anything to do with him again. I have also seen some say they no longer wish to be Christians because of the evils they see in the world, such as earthquakes and war.

Why does God let innocent people get killed in the war? These are questions we definitely, do not want to ask God. He is our maker, and how can you strive with your maker? Can the clay argue with

51

the potter for molding it into a kettle? Hmm! I wonder. I remember years ago, I used to listen to the news, and afterward, I would spend time crying so much that it sometimes became difficult to go out and function. I kept asking why. Why is there poverty in the world? Why did this tsunami happen and kill so many? Why are there diseases such as cancer and AIDS killing so many? Imagine if I continued to focus on this; it would have led me to depression because I felt so hurt for others.

Instead of dwelling on negative connotations, consider that if you believe in good and evil, you must also believe in God and the Devil! The Bible calls the devil the ruler of this world, and having caused man to fall, he gained control of the earth. So, when you see evil, it is because there is a devil at work. God, however, has given man free will, and man can do as they please, which is what we see as a result. God hardly intervenes in our affairs unless we ask him to do so through prayers and intercession.

God also says His ways are not our ways, and His thoughts differ from ours (Isaiah 55:8-9). He says He will show mercy to whom he will show mercy. Now, I don't know how other faiths really work, but I know the God in the Christian faith is gracious, merciful, and faithful. He loves us with an undying love that he gave his only son for us. He is the creator of the universe and causes the sun to shine on the good and the bad. The best way to walk with God to find inner peace is to believe what he says in the scriptures in

Jeremiah 29:11; "For I know the thoughts I think towards you, thoughts of good and not of evil. Thoughts to give you hope and a future."

If we believe this and in his promise of eternal life, we will have peace in our hearts, believing that he wishes us good, and when bad happens, he has got our back!

Chapter 3

The Power of Forgiveness

Letting Go of the Hurt

It is impossible to write a book about love without talking about forgiveness. Forgiveness is the prerequisite for demonstrating love in our relationships. The Cambridge Dictionary defines forgiveness as "to stop blaming or being angry with someone for what they have done or hurt they caused you." This is a very simplistic definition of a term that encompasses so many different aspects of our lives.

Forgiveness is an action or a feeling and, most times, a choice we make. Forgiveness can come in different forms, such as exoneration, forbearance, and release. Exoneration means wiping the slate and starting afresh, not remembering what happened. Forbearance requires patience, tolerance, and self-control. In this instance, you accept that what the individual did was wrong and that they might not even be remorseful, but you choose to forgive them. Release means making a conscious effort not to let the bitterness of the hurt take over and have its way in your life and over your relationships. Many of us have to forgive in the very many different relationships and loving environments in which we find ourselves. Parents forgive children and vice versa, husbands forgive wives and vice versa, friends forgive each other for wrongdoing, etc. The degree of forgiveness depends on the level of wrongdoing and the hurt we feel.

Forgiveness can be unilateral when we make the ultimate decision to forgive despite what the individual has done, even when they do not repent or show remorse. It can also be transactional, where we come to a mutual agreement to forgive because the person pleads for forgiveness or apologizes. The journey to inner peace requires a lot of unilateral forgiveness and letting go of things. This means forgiving the individual who hurt us, forgiving ourselves for the ill wishes we feel toward them and not counting the offense against them.

This is particularly important in our everyday relationships with our families, work colleagues, friends, etc. We sometimes fail to exercise forgiveness, leading to hatred, which can transcend generations. I have heard people say, "I will never forgive you." You cannot love someone you cannot forgive. Sometimes, forgiveness requires you to reconcile yourself with the individual, and sometimes it requires self-reconciliation.

Many get hurt and find it hard to love or trust again, so subsequent relationships suffer because they cannot forgive and forget. A caveat: it is somewhat easier to forgive, but forgetting might prove a tricky customer. If someone hurts you, there is a breach of trust, and we can say we forgive them, but when we remember the hurt, we don't feel like giving them another chance to hurt us again. For example, if someone steals from you, you can forgive them and accept their apologies, but it becomes tricky for us as humans to put them in that position of trust again.

Love, however, helps us to manage the hurt and helps us continue a clean slate. The Bible talks about turning the other cheek! This, I think, is the ultimate love. If someone hurts you or a member of your family, it requires you to look away. Imagine being punched in the face and turning the other cheek to get punched again! Hmm, that's a pretty hard one to do. If you can do this, you become the one with the ultimate power: the power of self-control.

In our relationships, we can fight and argue and quarrel, but the ultimate test of that relationship is the power to forgive each other's wrongdoings emotionally and physically.

I once saw a video about a woman whose son was murdered by a young man who then went to jail. While in jail, she visited the young man and reconciled with him. The most amazing part of this was the fact that after the young man left prison, she invited him to stay in her home and looked after him like her own son. They had such a close bond, and you could see the love they had for each other. This was, for me, the ultimate love. This was love born out of forgiveness. How do you love someone who murdered your son? Only the love of God can do this.

The love of God tells us about a God who is willing to die for us as humans because of the love he has for us.

The Bible says, *"Greater love hath no man than to lay his life down for his friend"* (John 15:13).

The only way he could do this was to forgive our sins and blot them out. God's type of forgiveness when you give your life to him means that he exonerates you completely of all the evil and bad things you have done in the past. He says, *"Old things have passed away, and all things have become new"* (2 Corinthians 5:17).

As I reflect on this, I think about how many of us truly forgive in our various relationships. As couples, we have misunderstandings and bring up old wounds, which then create new wounds, and then we struggle even more to forgive. Children need to learn to forgive the parent who abandoned or neglected them; parents need to forgive that wayward child who brought shame and disgrace to them and the family. Partners need to forgive their cheating spouses or spouses who do not meet their expectations, and most of all, we need to forgive ourselves and not remain in shame and despair.

Bitterness is what we are left with when we fail to forgive ourselves or others. We get angry with the world and with ourselves. Bitterness hampers our self-worth and makes us feel worthless. We then start to self-harm either by putting ourselves in danger with the lifestyle we choose or physically harming ourselves to distract us from the internal hurt we experience.

Yes, we made wrong decisions, and yes, we did wrong things or are still doing wrong things, such as drugs or alcohol, but if we make a conscious effort to forgive ourselves through self-love, we start to look forward to the future and start to make efforts to bring in real change to our current situations.

To achieve this kind of forgiveness, we need love. As I have previously said in scripture, love covers a multitude of sins, and according to biblical principles, love is long-suffering (1 Corinthians 13). To suffer long means you must continually forgive. Not every faith talks about forgiveness.

Some talk about vengeance and payback. If you kill someone who killed your child, how have they paid back? The child is still dead, and they are not living to feel any pain. It's an effort in futility. If forgiveness was practiced around the world in society, we would not hear about the wars we hear of today born out of the need for vengeance. Again, I refer to biblical principles: "Vengeance is mine, says the Lord." If God must be the judge and jury, then we must hand it over to him. We must let our minds be at peace, knowing that no matter how badly this person hurts us, they cannot live forever, and they are likely to face the ultimate judgment if they do not make restitution for their misdeeds.

In the Bible, Jesus was asked how many times one needed to forgive one's brother in a day, and he said, "70x7 times, i.e. 490 times! (Matthew 18.22) Imagine your brother actually offending you 490 times, phew! He must be a bad brother! On average, no one is likely to offend you 490 times in a day or even over time, although I am not sure if anyone is counting. I just feel we tend not to give anyone a chance to hurt us that much before we part ways with them.

On a more serious note, this tells us we can never stop forgiving. Our heavenly Father forgives us when we confess our sins, and he does not stop 490 times. He cleanses us completely, and it is only a matter of time before we realize that there are only so many times we can be forgiven for the same offense before we think of changing our ways. Even those in prison receive a pardon for heinous offenses if they can prove to have changed their ways.

I learned a lot about forgiveness as a Christian, and this has happened over time. I used to wonder how certain crimes could be forgiven, e.g., abuse of young children. I remember a friend of mine who had a friend who was a private teacher for her children. I later found out he was a previous child sex offender and had repented and become a

Christian. I found it hard to understand how my friend could forgive him enough to allow him to be near her children. She kept reminding me that when a person becomes born again, old things have passed away, and all things have become new (2 Corinthians 5:17).

Love makes us do so many things we struggle to do. Love makes a woman in an abusive marriage forgive her husband over and over again despite continuous beatings and abuse. Love makes children forgive their parents despite the neglect and abuse they faced when they were being brought up. Love makes us forgive our friends despite hurtful words or behaviors, including stabbing us in the back. Love makes us forgive our siblings, faith brothers, and sisters despite them not coming through for us when we need them to or shaming or slandering our name.

We often see avoiding people as forgiveness. We say to ourselves that we have forgiven them, but each time we see them or their pictures or anything relevant to them, we have this anxious knot in our stomach. When Jesus said, "Father, forgive them for they know not what they do" (Luke 23:34), he was not talking to people who just spoke badly about him. He was talking to people who physically brutalized him on the cross, nailed his hands and feet, spat at him, put a crown of thorns on his head, tore his garments, and cast lots over them. He demonstrated the ultimate love!

Chapter 4

Fear and the Unknown

A pastor of mine often defines fear as False Evidence Appearing Real. I think there is no better way to define fear because we are afraid of what we do not know. For example, when walking outside in the dark, we fear the things we cannot see or who might jump out on us from dark corners. In mental health, people with anxiety experience a lot of fear and panic—fear that someone will break into their houses or fear of what happens when they go out. This is false evidence because although things can happen to people when they are out, they are rare. However, the fear feels very real to the individual, and telling them this is not the case makes no sense.

The fear of the unknown in our relationships makes it difficult for us to give love fully in the relationship. When we start out in a friendship, we find it hard to be open or share intimate details with our newfound friends because we don't know how they would react to certain details about us, our backgrounds, or family life. This is fear of the unknown. We just don't know how people would react to us or who people really are. As humans, we often present the best of us in the early stages of relationships, and later, the flaws start to show themselves. Not knowing what to expect, we tend to become guarded. This presents itself in all our relationships, even our relationship with God. How can we love whom we do not see? How do we even know He exists? This is fear of the unknown, and the only way to develop this love for him is to build a relationship with Him. This is done through understanding his words as they are expressed in the Bible. The Bible helps us understand Him better, and when we know Him, we can express ourselves to Him and He to us. We start to know how much he loves us and what that love means, and we then start to see the evidence of that love all around us.

The Bible states in 1 John 4:18 that *"perfect love, cast out fear."* When we truly love, we stop entertaining fear—fear that our spouses might be cheating on us, fear that we are marrying into an unknown family and don't know if we would be accepted.

Don't get me wrong; sometimes, it is good to entertain some anxiety about certain things we do not know, such as a stranger offering us a lift. Hmm! That is one fear to entertain, as the evidence right in front of you is that the person is a stranger, and we do not know their intentions, and we have no one who can vouch for them at that moment.

It is also healthy to entertain anxiety before exams as we don't know what the questions are, but the adrenalin boost helps us to work harder. Seeing the end result of all our hard work in our heads before the exam is what helps us to overcome the fear. However, if you have not studied, be very afraid—I say this, laughing to myself. On a more serious note, having confidence in oneself and in God, who can help us in difficult situations, helps us overcome the fears we entertain because we see hope in the end.

We fear meeting the parents for the first time because we don't know how they would react or fear what to expect in our new jobs and how other staff would welcome or reject us. Children entertain fear of the unknown when they start a new school. You see them clinging to their parents and crying their eyes out, pleading for mum or dad not to let them enter this unfamiliar world. It is the not knowing that cripples our hearts and creates this fear. We fear starting our own business because we see in our heads so many pitfalls that have not even occurred.

The only way to conquer fear is not to see the mirage of evidence in front of us because there is no evidence there! It's all a figment of our imagination because it is not known, but it appears real. The most important thing is for us to have done all we can to ensure we have prepared for what we are going into and that the risks we are taking have been carefully considered.

The opposite of this is faith. Faith is the substance of things we are hoping for and the evidence of things we have not seen (Hebrews 11:1). It means everything we do is by faith. It is by faith that we get up and go to work or school because we believe we will be safe and that nothing evil will befall us on our way. That is faith because we don't know, but we trust the process. It is by faith that we get on an airplane, believing the pilot knows what he is doing and will land us safely at our destination. We don't know this, but it is the evidence we rely on in our heads. We think more about the beautiful destination we are going to in Dubai and the wonderful time we intend to have.

If we entertained fear, then we would never embark on that journey.

It is this same faith we must have when forming relationships, believing that we would love regardless and that things would always turn out for the better. If we were cynical, we would never have friends or relationships and would be isolated from the world. We must make a pact with ourselves to go in with the ultimate love regardless of what we see or think, and this will ensure we have peace in our hearts in every relationship. It is this love we must have in our hearts when wanting to give our lives to our unknown and unseen maker, believing he never lies and loves us unconditionally. Let us think about this when embarking on this wonderful journey to hope.

Chapter 5

Love Made This: The Ultimate You Designed to Love

Understanding the Ultimate Love

Understanding the ultimate love means understanding what it means to let go of hurt, shame, pain, bitterness, unforgiveness, and rejection. I go back to biblical principles and the word of God, which says if my father and mother reject me, the Lord will pick me up (Psalms 27:10), or the word that says He is the Father to the fatherless (Psalms 68:5).

It is easy to remain bitter, wallow in self-pity, and believe nobody loves you. You throw a pity party for yourself, and it almost feels like the pain is pleasurable. However, it holds you back and prevents you from functioning or coping with life. I once dealt with someone who had lost a parent, and four years down the line, despite counseling and every other possible intervention, they were unable to let go of the pain of bereavement. This demonstrates that the key to experiencing ultimate love is to leave the pain behind and move towards a more hopeful future. This is more difficult for some than others, but it must be intentional on our part. Yes, our mother or father neglected us as children, and then we hold on to that and neglect our children. What the ultimate love does is to give us that inner peace. It helps us to let go and let God.

There is a scripture in the Bible that says, "The Lord will keep in perfect peace those whose mind is stay focused on Him." If you focus your mind on the word of God and use that to dispel that voice in your head that keeps reminding you of how someone broke your heart or how disappointed you feel about their actions, then you will never break that yoke holding you to negativity. You can achieve ultimate love by looking at the definition of love according to **1 Corinthians 13** in the Bible:

"Love suffers long and is kind; Love does not envy; Love does not parade itself, is not [b]puffed up; 5 does not behave rudely, does not seek its own, is not provoked, [c]thinks no evil; 6 does not rejoice in iniquity, but rejoices in the truth; 7 bears all things, believes all things, hopes all things, endures all things."

Imagine you were long-suffering in a marriage or a friendship or in your church; you build resilience, and nothing faces you. Imagine you were always kind to others, and people will feel the need to gravitate to you and listen to what you have to say when you say it in love. Imagine you were not proud and arrogant, and you humbled yourself and did not display narcissistic behavior.

What would it really look like for you? Imagine you were even-tempered and did not throw temper tantrums and outbursts of rage (I have worked with so many with this difficulty, and all they want is not to be like this, so they avoid people and going out because they might become outraged for a little thing and do or say the wrong thing. Imagine they understood how to be more enduring of other's faults and imagine parents being more hopeful that their children will turn out right despite what they see.

The ultimate love is the love of Jesus. This helps us to react in the way love is described above. The Bible again states that we should hide His word in our hearts, which then helps us avoid sin. This means if we are about to hurt someone, we think of His word, which says we must love one another and be kind to one another or ask us to forgive those who offend us. This refrains us from doing something bad or evil.

Now, I know this is a process we all must go through over time to find this inner peace. I am still on that journey, and when I reflect and look back, I see how far I have come from the frustrations I faced that led to outbursts of anger and rage for little things to where I am now. Now, I constantly remind myself that people are human and deserve love regardless, so I must forgive them and find a way to see the good in them. This is my journey so far, and it has taken away hurt and provided me with peace —peace when I feel I have given so much and not getting much in return, peace when I feel I deserve love from someone I love so much, and I don't get it back, and peace when I feel offended or disappointed by my Christian brother or sister and still continue to love God and love them. The word of God says we will face tribulations in this world, but He has overcome the world and offers us peace that surpasses understanding (John 16.33). Is this not the best emotional state to be in?

The New Refreshed You

Wow, welcome to the new, refreshed you—the you that can withstand hurt, pain, and shame. The you that is moving forward, despite all the hardships in life, because you have hope and know all will be well. Welcome to that new you who loves unconditionally, forgives immediately, and does not hold a grudge. Welcome to the you that feels happy, peaceful, joyful, and willing to let things slide.

The new, refreshed you has the ultimate self-love because you have decided to love yourself and not let hurt take over. You have decided to live at peace with all men and not let them steal your joy. You have decided to move on with life and form relationships without getting hung up on past hurts. The real you is striving to forgive your parents for abandoning you. The real you is trying to forgive your husband for cheating on you and not holding on to that in your heart. The real you forgive your workmates for being so nasty to you at work and pray for them! This is what the Bible describes as the fruit of the spirit in

Galatians 5:22: *"Love, joy, peace, longsuffering, kindness, goodness, faithfulness, 23 gentleness, self-control. Against such, there is no law."*

Thinking about this, I have not seen a law that accuses you of committing an offense for being good, gentle, loving, kind or exercising self-control. There are laws against the opposite. If you get angry, start shouting or attacking someone, you can be arrested for assault!

Therefore, let go and let love, the very agape love which can heal you of every hurt.

Conclusion

I hope this book has helped you start on the journey of healing and has given you insight into what love means and how it can transform your life.

We have examined the various definitions of love and how this can help us put love in perspective. We have also examined the various difficulties experienced in love and how important it is for us to be intentional about our choice to love and find that inner peace we so desire.

We have explored unforgiveness and how it can hinder our lives and cause us to remain static and unproductive. Remember, when you don't forgive, you bear the burden and the pain. The other party is probably moving on with their lives, happy with the new thing they have discovered that is giving them joy, while you remain in bitterness and carry the weight all the days of your life. A question I prefer to ask myself is: Is it worth it?

Finally, I want to be the new you. Do you want to be the new you and experience this peacefulness with Love in your heart toward people? Then make a pact with me today and agree to start on this new journey of self-discovery and the ultimate Love of God, which will give you peace no one can understand and make beautiful family relationships happen. Join me on this journey.

Please reach out and tell me if you have embarked on this journey with me or leave a review and help someone else go on this journey of healing.

Yours in Love, K. Emmanuel

About the Author

The author is a minister, a professional Mental Health Nurse, a teacher, and a businesswoman. She is married with three children and has spent her lifetime serving God in various capacities in ministry. She is one of four siblings and is an aunt to many nephews and nieces.

In her profession as a Mental Health Nurse, she has experienced relationship breakdowns herself and managed many individuals experiencing mental health difficulties due to such breakdowns, in addition to counseling and supporting individuals with practical tools for managing their relationships.

She is passionate about helping people thrive and managing their hurt so that they can lead healthy, peaceful, joyful, and fulfilled lifestyles.

References

Burton, N. (2024, July 19). These Are the 7 Types of Love. Psychology Today. Retrieved July 23, 2024, from https://www.psychologytoday.com/us/blog/hide-and-seek/201606/these-are-the-7-types-of-love

Cherry, K. (2023, February 22). Attachment Theory: Bowlby and Ainsworth's Theory Explained. Verywell Mind. Retrieved July 28, 2024, from https://www.verywellmind.com/what-is-attachment-theory-2795337

Mcleod, S. (2024, January 17). Attachment Theory In Psychology Explained. Simply Psychology. Retrieved July 23, 2024, from https://www.simplypsychology.org/attachment.html

Regan, S. (2022, December 28). 8 Types Of Love + How To Find Out Which One You Have. MindBodyGreen. Retrieved July 23, 2024, from https://www.mindbodygreen.com/articles/types-of-love

Book Review

Keeping the Game of Love Alive

Now that you have learned so much about love and how to keep it strong, it's time to share what you've discovered with others who need this wisdom too.

Simply by leaving your honest opinion of this book, you'll guide other readers, just like you, to the help they are looking for. Your review will help other adults in relationships find the inspiration and advice they need from "LOVE MADE THIS HAPPEN" and pass on this message of love.

Thank you for your help. The journey of love is kept alive when we share our knowledge and experiences – and you're helping me to do just that.

Thank you from the bottom of my heart.

Your biggest fan,

Kemi Emmanuel

Email: K.emmanuel2024@yahoo.com